TROLL

Th. Kittelsen.

EDITOR

PER ERIK BORGE

EAST OF THE SUN
AND WEST OF THE MOON

Norwegian trolls and fairytales

Who has never seen a troll during a nocturnal walk in the dark forest? A tousled head appearing from behind a large crag, or a gleaming troll eye shining between heavy tree trunks. In no other Scandinavian countries are trolls such an established part of the culture and the narrative tradition as in Norway. Quite literally, trolls loom large in folklore and fairytales. But why particularly in Norway? There are several explanations.

«In an overpopulated Europe, Norway is still Nature's kingdom. Deep inside the endless forests, silence prevails as it has for thousands of years. In there, modern life counts for nothing. The silence in the face of Nature's powerful rhythm leaves modern man, who counts his piecemeal existence in hours and minutes, feeling rather helpless. The huge forest sings its eternal hymn. A grey-bearded tree comes crashing down with old age, to lie as if felled by the wind between new shoots, new trees. The seasons come and go, summer and winter, spring and autumn, in inevitable repetition. Eternity prevails.

In there live the trolls. The troll is Norwegian, the natural spirit of the Norwegian forests. He is not fleet of foot like the Greek faun, which capered over bare, sun-drenched hills. He is heavy, dark and overgrown. He is a walking forest and mountain.

In these pertinent words from his book published in 1974, Kittelsen's biographer Odd Hølaas identifies some of the most characteristic features of Norwegian troll stories. They effectively echo what every Norwegian feels for the huge, heavy fir woods that clothe Norway in their dark-green cloak. Hølaas calls this our fear of nature, fear of the forests, an ingrained fear of the dark which we have never grown out of. Norwegian nature is an inexhaustible source of new fairytale fantasies and stories about trolls.

Moreover, the happy combination of folk tradition and Theodor Kittelsen's creativeness as an illustrator has produced troll figures that are as familiar to Norwegians as their evening prayers and goat's milk cheese. These strange moss-covered, twisted creatures, roaming at night or still as stone, have become part of Norwegian culture. Every Norwegian knows what the trolls of Hedal Forest look like, or the three-headed troll who imprisons the princess in the blue mountain. Kittelsen has depicted them for us, and we never forget them.

Few Norwegian illustrators or painters have managed to capture these strange creatures and the enchanted atmosphere of Norwegian nature on paper or canvas as successfully as Theodor Kittelsen. Kittelsen's artistic use of the medium of drawing, with black and white extremities and scales of grey in between, are in a class of their own in Norwegian art.

From folktales, trolls found their way into literature. When Henrik Ibsen wanted to portray the dark side of the Norwegian character in his play Peer Gynt, he employed trolls. When the Mountain King asks Peer Gynt what the difference is between man and troll, and the avaricious and ambitious Peer unhesitatingly replies that it is very little, the Mountain King retorts:

«Among men, the saying goes: 'Man, to yourself be true!' In here, among us trolls, the saying runs: 'Troll, to yourself be - enough!'»

Peer Gynt makes a pact with the spirits and pays the price. However, there is also a certain kindliness about Norwegian trolls. They are terrifying and powerful, but also stupid and easily overpowered by an agile, quick-witted youth or a brave soldier. We therefore read the stories with a mixture of fear and delight. They always end happily for the disobedient human being who stands up to the trolls, and contain plenty of homely wit, good-natured fantasy and humour.

The origins of these fairytales are difficult to pinpoint today. Legends and fairytales migrate between countries and continents. Everywhere they take hold, they acquire their own local colouring and linguistic form. In Norway, fairytales were undoubtedly combined with Old Norse legends and similar motifs from the heroic sagas.

Even though the history of folktales can be traced back a long way, it was not until last century that any of them were written down. Until then, fairytales had been regarded as popular culture, the preserve of the common people. The great Ludvig Holberg, Copenhagen's poet from Bergen, dismissed folklore as old wives' tales. But when the tide of Romanticism began to sweep across Europe in the early 19th century, popular culture was dusted down and worshipped by artists, writers and composers.

In philosophical terms, Romanticism was a reaction against the 18th century's stubborn belief in reason. Romanticism emphasised the imagination, emotions and subjective intensity, and was therefore a fertile breeding ground for nationalist movements that made much of national characteristics. Historical and linguistic research took on new directions, and the study of popular customs, coupled with the collection of fairytales and folksongs, was established.

This is the contemporary European background against which Norway's two collectors of folklore, Peter Christen Asbjørnsen and Jørgen Moe, carried out their work, undoubtedly inspired and influenced by the brothers Jacob and Wilhelm Grimm in Germany, and by their contemporary Hans Christian Andersen in Denmark.

Asbjørnsen and Moe's Norwegian fairytales were first published in the early 1840s. Later they appeared in a collected edition, profusely illustrated by the best artists of the time, among them Theodor Kittelsen and Erik Werenskiold. Asbjørnsen and Moe did not write down the stories exactly as they were told to them in terms of either language or content. They collected the stories and retold them, which meant for instance that the type of language changed, even though they sought to produce «a faithful rendering of what was related to us by the storyteller».

With their collections of folktales, principally from eastern Norway, they laid the foundations for part of our cultural heritage which is nowadays shared by all Norwegians. Both the language and the motifs of the stories have passed into everyday patterns of speech and thought. Folktales and forest trolls have become part of daily life in both urban and rural Norway.

The excerpts from fairytales contained in this book are mainly what are known as fantastic or magical tales, which are the most common type of

Norwegian folktale. These stories usually deal with trolls, witches and people with supernatural powers. For instance, Askeladden has seven-mile boots and manages to eat an unlimited amount of food, while golden castles glitter and entice people into the mountain where a troll is keeping a princess captive, and Veslefrikk is given an enchanted fiddle by a poor man which makes every living creature dance.

We have also included in the book Theodor Kittelsen's own descriptions of particular creatures from fairytales and legends such as the waterfall spirit, the pixie and the goblins, also referred to as fairies. Goblins are small, grey-clad beings who are jealous of the ability of humans to live in the sunlight. Fairies often appear to tempt or threaten people, and inhabit a world that is very similar to the human world, with cattle and farms, fishing and boats on the lake.

Theodor Kittelsen was fascinated by this shadowy world populated by supernatural siren beings and spirits. Walking in the forests and fields, he could see them everywhere: in the mists over the marshes, in the twilight surrounding fallen pine trunks and in the dripping fir trees on rainy days. And when the family were safely tucked up in bed, they might well hear the house spirits, or pixies, rummaging in the kitchen or outhouse.

The Norwegian painter Christian Krogh wrote of Kittelsen's relationship with Norwegian fairytales and trolls that «we are captivated and enticed into a whole new world, where we feel, suffer and observe with him, this intense man, who ventures alone with open eyes and receptive nerves into immense, pure, untamed Nature».

THE FOREST TROLL

The woods, the wild monotony of the woods, has left its mark on us, we have become one with Nature. We love it for what it is, with its melancholy power.

As children, we used to stare up into the rustling fir and pine trees, following their mighty trunks with our eyes and our soul. We climbed about in the strong, twisted branches, until we reached the very tops - the swaying, rustling treetops, up there in the beautiful blue.

When the sun set, solitude and peace descended over the great woods, a dense silence. It was as if they dared not breathe, as if the woods were lying in quiet, silent expectation. Then our hearts would pound. We wanted more - we begged and pleaded for adventures, exciting, wild adventures for us poor children.

And the forest gave us an adventure.

Large but quiet, it approached stealthily, like the soft, soundless tread of a cat.

Everything that had been as immobile as stone began to move.

In the distance, a rock moved, inspiring awe and fear. It acquired eyes, started moving, walked in immobile silence straight towards us. And we rejoiced in our fear, we loved it!

It was the forest troll. His single eye revealed all the horror and fear, all the gold and glistening glamour our childish fantasy demanded.

We wanted to be terrified, and we wanted to stand up to him. Small though we were, we wanted to tease him, hack at his heels and steal his gold. But most of all, we wanted the shining eye from his forehead. Who would have believed that the ugly forest troll would possess such an eye?

THE SMALL BOYS
WHO MET THE TROLLS OF
HEDAL FOREST

Shortly after bedding down, they heard someone snorting and breathing heavily. The boys pricked up their ears, listening to see whether it was an animal or a forest troll they could hear. Then the breathing came closer and closer and the creature said:

«I smell the blood of a Christian!» Then they heard footsteps so heavy that the earth shook, which told them there were trolls about.

«God help us, what are we to do?» the younger boy asked his brother.

«Well, you stay where you are under the pine tree, and be ready to grab the bags and run away when you see them coming, and I'll take the small axe,» said the other boy.

At that moment they saw the trolls approaching. They were so big and heavy that their heads were level with the tops of the pine trees. But they had only one eye between the three of them, which they took turns to use. They had a hole in their forehead in which to place it, moving it with their hands. The troll in front had to have the eye, while the others walked behind, holding on to the leader.

«Take to your heels,» said the elder boy, but don't run too far until you see how it's going. Because their eye is so high up, they'll find it hard to see me when I come up behind them.

So his brother ran on ahead, and the trolls chased him. Meanwhile, the elder boy came up behind them and struck the hindmost troll on the ankle, so that it let out a terrible scream. The leading troll was so frightened and startled that it dropped the eye, which the boy lost no time in picking up. It was bigger than two dishes put together, and so bright that even the pitch-black night seemed like broad daylight when he looked through it.

THE THREE PRINCESSES IN
THE BLUE MOUNTAIN

Suddenly the troll appro-
ached very fast, making the
castle shake.

«Ho, ho! I smell the
blood and bones of a Christian in my
house,» he said.

«Yes, a raven just flew over with a
human bone in his beak, which he
dropped down the chimney. Although
I threw it away and cleaned up carefully
afterwards, I'm sure you can still smell it.»

«I knew it,» said the troll.

«But come and I'll delouse you,» said
the princess, «then it should be better
when you wake up.»

The troll immediately agreed to
this, and before long he had fallen asleep
and was snoring. When she noticed that
he was asleep, she placed chairs and
eiderdowns under his heads and went
out to call the hens. Then the soldier
sneaked inside, drew his sword and cut
off all the troll's three heads in a single
stroke.

THE GOLDEN BIRD

When they came to the troll with the horse, they took both the horse and the finest bridle, and when they came to the troll with the linden tree and the bird, they took both the linden tree and the bird and made off with them.

When they had been travelling like this for a while, they came to a field of rye, and the fox said, «I can hear a noise. You carry on alone, I'll stay here for a bit.» Then he made himself a coat of rye, which made him look as if he was standing there preaching. Suddenly all three trolls came running along, thinking they were going to catch up with them.

«Have you seen anyone passing by with a beautiful maiden, a horse with a golden bridle, a golden bird and a gilded linden tree?» they called to the man standing preaching.

«Yes, my great-great-grandmother told me a procession like that had passed by here, but that was in the good old days, when her great-great-grandmother used to bake shilling buns and sell two for one shilling, and give the shilling back.»

The trolls burst into a fit of laughter. «Ha, ha, ha, ha!» they cried, putting their arms round one another. «If we've been asleep that long, we may as well turn round and go home to bed,» they said, before leaving the same way they had come.

The boy took the old woman under one arm and the sack under the other and made off with them. «You see now, we're not far from where people live. Look at those bright lights,» said the boy.

But the old woman said those were not people, they were mountain trolls, for she knew the whole forest, and she knew there were no people there, the nearest being on the other side of the hill to the north.

When they had walked a little way, they came to a big, red-painted farm.

«We mustn't go inside,» said the old woman. «Mountain trolls live here.»

«Oh yes, we're going inside. See, there are lights, there must be people in there,» replied the boy. He went in first, and the old woman followed, but as soon as he opened the door she fainted, because she had seen a big fat man sitting on a stool.

«Good evening, grandfather,» said the boy.

«I've been sitting here for three hundred years now, but no-one has ever called me grandfather,» said the man sitting on the stool.

The boy sat down beside the man and started talking to him as if they were old acquaintances.

«But what happened to your mother?» asked the man, after they had been talking for a while. «I think she fainted, you'd better see if she's all right.»

The boy went out, picked up the old woman and dragged her across the floor. Then she came to, crawled away and sat hiding in the corner where the firewood was kept, but she was so scared that she hardly dared peek out.

Th. Kittelsen

VESLEFRIKK AND HIS FIDDLE

Veslefrikk walked on for a while, until he grew tired and sat down to rest, and when he was seated comfortably, a poor man came up to him again. He was so big and tall and ugly that the boy had to keep looking higher and higher, right up into the sky, and when he finally saw how big and ugly and ragged the man was, he began crying.

«Don't be afraid of me, my boy,» said the man. «I won't do you any harm, I'm just a poor man asking for a shilling in God's name.»

«Believe me,» said Veslefrikk, «I have only one shilling left, and I'm on my way to town to buy clothes with that. If I had met you earlier, then ...»

«Yes, but I have not a single shilling, and a bigger body and fewer clothes, so I am worse off than you,» said the poor man.

So Veslefrikk let him have the shilling, there was nothing else for it. Then each had something and he had nothing.

«Well, since you have such a kind heart that you have given away everything you possessed,» said the poor man, «I will grant you one wish for each shilling.» The same poor man had taken all three of them. He had simply changed his shape each time so that the boy would not recognise him.

«I always have such a longing to hear the sound of a fiddle, and to see people dancing so merrily and gaily,» replied the boy. «So if I can wish for anything I like, then I wish for a fiddle which every living creature must dance to,» he said.

THE FAIRIES

In the old days, everywhere teemed with fairies. From mounds and hillocks came the sound of fiddle music and dancing, and sometimes a long bridal procession of little men and women dressed in grey would pass by. They used to come with a golden horn and cup and invite those present to drink. But woe betide anyone who drank, for then he was in their power.

As soon as twilight fell, the grey folk would creep forth, and then it was dangerous to be outside, especially for young girls. Many a beautiful girl used to be tempted inside a hill or mountain, after which she would go about half mad, talking about her rich suitors with their fine cattle and big farms.

ASKELADDEN STEALS
THE TROLL'S PIECES OF SILVER,
BEDSPREAD AND GOLDEN HARP

The King told the boy that his brother had said he claimed to be able to steal the troll's bedspread with silver and golden squares in it, and that he was now to do so, otherwise he would forfeit his life. Askeladden replied that he had neither said nor thought any such thing, but it was no use, so he asked for three days in which to think about it. When the three days were up, he rowed across in the kneading trough and walked up and down while he waited. Finally he saw them hanging out the bedspread on the mountainside to air it, and when they had safely disappeared back into the mountain, Askeladden stole it and rowed away as fast as he could.

When he was half way across, the troll came out and saw him.

«Was it you who stole my seven pieces of silver?» shouted the troll.

«Ye-es,» replied the boy.

«Did you also take my bedspread, with one silver square and one golden square and one silver square and one golden square in it?»

«Ye-es,» said the boy.

«Will you come back again?»

«Quite possibly,» answered the boy.

When he returned to the palace with the golden and silver bedspread, everyone liked him even better than before, and he became the King's personal servant.

"Er det du som har tat de
syv Sölvanderne mine?"

Th. Kittel

SORIA MORIA CASTLE

The fire was burning in the castle, and Halvor entered the kitchen, which was the finest kitchen he had ever seen. There were vessels made of gold and silver, but there was no-one there. After he had stood there for a while, and nobody appeared, he went over to a door and turned the handle. Inside, a princess sat spinning at a wheel.

«Well, well,» she cried, «do Christian folk dare to set foot here? It would probably be best if you went away, otherwise the troll will gobble you up, for a troll with three heads lives here.

«I don't mind if he has four, I should still like to see the fellow,» said the boy, «and I'm not leaving, for I have done nothing wrong. But you must give me some food, because I'm terribly hungry.»

When Halvor had had enough to eat, the princess told him to see if he could swing the sword that was hanging on the wall. But he could not swing it, he was not even able to lift it.

«Well,» said the princess, «then you must drink a mouthful from the bottle hanging beside it, which is what the troll does when he wants to go out and use the sword.»

Halvor drank a mouthful and was immediately able to swing the sword without difficulty. Now, he thought, it was time for the troll to appear.

Just then, the troll approached rapidly. Halvor was behind the door.

«Fe fi fo, I smell the blood of a Christian!» cried the troll, sticking his head through the door.

«Yes, you can indeed,» answered Halvor, chopping off the troll's head.

The princess was so happy to be rescued that she danced and sang.

ASKELADDEN'S EATING
CONTEST WITH THE TROLL

After Askeladden had been chopping wood for a little while, the troll came up to him and said:

«If you're chopping down my forest, I'll kill you!»

The boy was quick off the mark. He ran off into the forest to fetch the cheese his mother had put in his bag of provisions, which he squeezed until the whey ran out. «If you don't keep quiet,» he shouted to the troll, I'll squeeze you the way I'm squeezing the water out of this white stone!»

«Oh, please spare me,» said the troll, «and I'll help you chop wood.»

So on that condition the boy spared him, and the troll was good at chopping, so that day they managed to fell and chop dozens of trees.

As evening approached, the troll said, «Now you can come home with me, for my home is nearer than yours.»

So the boy accompanied him, and when they came to the troll's home, the troll intended to make up the fire, while the boy went to fetch water for making porridge. But the two iron pails standing there were so heavy that he could not even lift them.

So the boy said, «It's not worth taking these thimbles. I'll go and fetch the whole well!»

«No, my friend,» replied the troll, «I can't do without my well. You make up the fire, and I'll go and fetch the water.»

When he returned with the water, they brewed up a goodly amount of porridge.

«It's all the same to me,» said the boy, «but if you like, we can have an eating contest.»

«Oh yes!,» replied the troll, who believed he would easily win.

So they sat down to eat, but the boy surreptitiously picked up his leather bag and tied it in front of him, then he poured more porridge into the bag than he ate himself. When the bag was full, he took out his pocket knife and cut a slit in the bag. The troll watched him but said nothing.

After they had been eating for a good while longer, the troll put down his spoon. «Well, I can't manage any more,» he said.

«You must eat more!» answered the boy, «I'm not even half full yet. If you do as I did, and cut a hole in your stomach, then you can eat as much as you like.»

«But isn't that terribly painful?» asked the troll.

«Oh, nothing to speak of,» the boy replied.

So the troll did as the boy said and, as you can imagine, he killed himself. But the boy took all the silver and gold in the mountain and returned home. And after that, he was always able to pay off his debts.

POLAR BEAR
KING VALEMON

On the evening of the third Thursday, the polar bear returned. Then he fought even harder than previously, and the King realised he could not let him defeat the entire army, so he gave him the third daughter in God's name. So he took her on his back and travelled far and further than far, and when they had entered the forest he asked her, as he had asked her two sisters, whether she had ever sat more comfortably and seen more clearly.

«No, never,» she replied.

«Well, you're the right one,» he said. Then they came to a castle, which was so splendid that her father's castle seemed like the most miserable hovel in comparison. Here she was to live, and live well, and she would have nothing to do apart from ensuring that the fire never went out. The bear would be away during the day, but at night he would be with her, and then he would be human.

THE PIXIE

The pixie is a funny little creature. He has only four fingers on each hand, and no thumbs. But it is probably best to stay friends with him all the same. With his eight crooked fingers, he has seized many a fellow and given him a good thrashing, leaving him a cripple for the rest of his life. Otherwise the pixie is not too bad, as long as he gets his beloved porridge, which he has to have.

And porridge with a dab of butter is reasonable payment for all his hard work. He looks after the cows and keeps an eye on the horses, steals hay and corn from the neighbouring farm, and generally does his best on behalf of the farmer he lives with. A farm without a pixie is not worth much.

But he is a great one for playing jokes. Everywhere, in the hayloft and the barn, you can hear him sniggering and giggling and gloating. Usually he sits on the barn bridge in the moonlight, dangling his legs over the edge. Then he vanishes suddenly every now and again, to pinch the cat's heels or tease the farmyard dog. (…)

At night, it is not pleasant to lie listening to the pixie. Sometimes there is a gentle sound like a ball, then things start whistling and hissing, until suddenly there is a terrible commotion: tin buckets fall to the floor, empty jars and bottles come tumbling down, and all around there are tiny footsteps, like a hundred rat feet. Then, suddenly, all is quiet again. And so he can carry on all night. It is hardly surprising that most people have no wish to get up wearing only their nightshirt and clamber up into the loft to see what is going on.

PEER GYNT IN THE HALL OF THE MOUNTAIN KING

Mountain King:

Cool it! (Beckons his courtiers to come closer) Don't let's boast. We've gone downhill in recent years; we no longer know if we'll make a go of things, and public assistance is not to be sneered at. What's more, this lad is quite without fault, and well built too, as far as I can see.

True, he has only one head; but my daughter has no more than that herself. Three-headed trolls have gone completely out of fashion; and you scarcely even set eyes on a two-headed one; and the heads you do see are only so-so. (To Peer Gynt) So you're after my daughter, then?

Peer Gynt:

Your daughter and your kingdom as a dowry, yes.

Mountain King:

You'll get half of it while I'm still alive and the other half when I die.

Peer Gynt:

I'll be happy with that.

Mountain King:

But wait a minute, my boy - You've got to make some promises too. If you break any of them, the whole pact is off, and you won't get out of here alive. First, you must promise that you will never take any notice of what goes on outside Rondane's borders; you are to shun daylight and its deeds and any speck of light.

Peer Gynt:

That's well worth it for the sake of a king's title.

BUTTERBALL

Once upon a time there was an old woman who sat at home baking. She had a small boy who was so fat and hefty and so fond of good food that she called him Butterball. She also had a dog called Goldtooth. Suddenly the dog started barking.

«Run outside, Butterball, and see who Goldtooth is barking at.»

So the boy ran outside, then came back in and said: «God help me, a big, tall troll-hag is coming with her head under her arm and a sack on her back.»

«Run and hide under the pastry board,» his mother said.

Then the big troll entered.
«Good day!» she said.
«God bless!» said Butterball's mother.

«Is Butterball at home today?» asked the troll.

«No, he's in the woods hunting grouse with his father,» his mother replied.

«That's a nuisance,» said the troll-hag, «I've got a nice little silver knife I wanted to give him.»

«Peep, peep, here I am!» cried Butterball, emerging from under the pastry board.

«I'm so old my back is stiff,» said the troll. «You can crawl inside my sack and find it for yourself.»

Once Butterball had got safely inside, the troll slung the sack over her shoulder and made for the door. But after they had travelled a little way, the troll became tired and asked, «How far is it to a resting place?»

«Half a quarter-mile,» replied Butterball.

So the troll put down the sack, went off into the wood by herself and lay down to sleep. Meanwhile, Butterball made sure it was safe, then took out his knife, cut a hole in the sack and crawled out, putting a large pine root in his place, before running home to his mother. When the troll got home and saw what she had in the sack, she was terribly angry.

The next day, the old woman was baking again. Suddenly the dog started barking.

«Run outside, Butterball, and see who Goldtooth is barking at.»

«Oh no, oh no!» cried Butterball. «It's that evil beast again, with her head under her arm and a big sack on her back.»

«Run and hide under the pastry board,» his mother said.

«Good day!» said the troll. «Is Butterball at home today?»

«No, he isn't,» said his mother. «He's in the woods hunting grouse with his father.»

«That's a nuisance,» said the troll-hag, «I've got a nice little silver fork I wanted to give him.»

«Peep, peep, here I am!» cried Butterball, stepping forward.

«I'm so old my back is stiff,» said the troll. «You can crawl inside my sack and find it for yourself.» Once

Butterball had got safely inside, the troll slung the sack over her shoulder and made off.

After they had travelled a little way, the troll became tired and asked, «How far is it to a resting place?»

«Half a mile,» replied Butterball. So the troll put down the sack, went off into the forest and lay down to sleep. While the troll was doing this, Butterball cut a hole in the sack and crawled out, then put a big stone inside the sack. When the troll-hag got home, she made up the fire, placed an enormous pot over it and prepared to boil Butterball. But when she picked up the sack ready to let Butterball out, the stone fell out and made a hole in the bottom of the pot, so that the water ran out and extinguished the fire. Then the troll became angry and said, «No matter what mischief he gets up to, I'll trick him yet.»

The same thing happened the third time. Goldtooth started barking, and mother said to Butterball, «Run outside, Butterball, and see who Goldtooth is barking at.»

Butterball ran outside and came back in crying, «Oh, woe is me! It's the troll again, with her head under her arm and a sack on her back.»

«Run and hide under the pastry board,» his mother said.

«Good day!» said the troll, as she

came through the door. «Is Butterball at home today?»

«No, he isn't,» said his mother. «He's in the woods hunting grouse with his father.»

«That's a nuisance,» said the troll-hag, «I've got a nice little silver spoon I wanted to give him.»

«Peep, peep, here I am!» cried Butterball, emerging from under the pastry board.

«I'm so old my back is stiff,» said the troll-hag. «You can crawl inside my sack and find it for yourself.»

Once Butterball had got safely inside, the troll slung the sack over her shoulder and made off. This time she did not go off by herself to rest, but went straight home with Butterball in the sack, and when they arrived it was Sunday.

Then the troll said to her daughter: «You take Butterball and kill him and make him into broth before I come back. I'm going to church to invite people to a feast.»

Once the old hag had left, her daughter was supposed to take Butterball and kill him, but she was not sure how to do it.

«Oh, I can easily show you what to do,» said Butterball. «Put your head on the bench and watch.»

The poor creature did this, and Butterball picked up an axe and chop-

ped off her head, as if she were a chicken. Then he put her head in the bed and her body in the pot, and made the troll's daughter into broth. When he had done this, he clambered above the door, carrying the pine root and the stone, and placed one over the door and the other on top of the troll's chimney.

When the people returned from church and saw the head in the bed, they thought the daughter was asleep. Then they went to taste the broth.

«Tastes delicious, Butterball-broth!» said the hag.

«Tastes delicious, daughter-broth!» called Butterball from the chimney.

They wondered who was speaking and went outside to see. But when they came out of the door, Butterball threw the pine root and the stone at their heads and killed them. Then he took all the gold and silver in the house, which made him very rich, and went home to his mother.

THE WATER-SPRITE

The water-sprite is cunning. Humans are his prey. When the sun sets, you must beware. He could be lying under the large, shining water-lily that you reach for with your hand. The moment you touch it, the quagmire will give way beneath you, and he will grasp you with

his wet, slimy hands. Or when you are sitting alone by the pond one evening - memories rise to the surface, at first one by one, then whole hosts of memories with the same warmth and radiance as the reflected sunlight between the leaves and the water-lilies. Watch yourself! The water-sprite is playing with your feelings. The pond conjures forth the memories, and the water-sprite lies in wait beneath. He knows how easy it is to trap us in its beautiful, quivering reflections.

THE HEN DANCING IN THE MOUNTAIN

Mother sat at home waiting and waiting, but her daughter did not return. She waited for a good while longer, but having neither heard nor seen any sign of her, she told her middle daughter to go out and look for her sister, and to call the hen at the same time.

So the second sister went out, and exactly the same thing happened to her: she looked for the hen and called it, and suddenly she too heard a voice from the cliff:

«The hen is dancing in the mountain! The hen is dancing in the mountain!»

She thought this was very strange and went to see what it was. Then she too fell through the trapdoor, deep, deep into the vaults. She walked through all the rooms, and in the innermost room the troll appeared and asked if she would be his beloved. No, she certainly would not, she wanted to go straight back up to search for the missing hen. Then the troll grew angry. He seized her, twisted her head off, and threw her head and body down into the cellar.

So when the woman had been sitting waiting for her second daughter too for seven lengths and seven breadths, and having neither heard nor seen her, she said to her youngest daughter:

«Now you must go out and look for your sisters. Though it's a pity the hen went missing, it would be even worse if we didn't find your sisters, but you can always call the hen at the same time.

So the youngest sister went out. She walked hither and thither, searching and calling, but she could not see the hen and she could not see her sisters. After a long time she too came to the cliff, and then she heard a voice:

«The hen is dancing in the mountain! The hen is dancing in the mountain!»

She thought this was very strange and went to see what it was. Then she too fell through the trapdoor, deep, deep into the vaults. Once down there, she walked from room to room, each more splendid than the last. But she was not afraid, she took her time looking at one thing and another, and then she caught sight of the trapdoor leading to the cellar. She looked into it and immediately recognised her sisters lying there.

Just as she was closing the trapdoor, the troll appeared. «Will you be my beloved?» asked the troll.

«Yes, gladly,» replied the girl, easily guessing what had happened to her sisters.

When the troll heard this, he gave her fine, fine clothes, the finest she could wish for, and everything else she desired, so happy was the troll that someone wanted to be his beloved.

RED FOX AND ASKELADDEN

«Yes, blind man's buff! Wouldn't you like to play blind man's buff?» asked Askeladden. Well, that might be fun, thought the troll. «But you go first,» he told Askeladden. «Yes, gladly,» said the boy. «But it's best if we count, then we shan't have anything to quarrel over.»

So that is what they did and, as you might guess, Askeladden made sure the troll put on the blindfold and took the first turn. But you should have seen them playing blind man's buff! They ran about on the edge of the forest, the troll stumbling and blundering into the tree stumps, so that the touchwood crackled and sparks flew.

«Ow, ow, I'm damned if I'm playing the blind man any more!» cried the troll, who was so angry. «Wait a moment,» said Askeladden, «I'll stand still and call out when you catch me.»

Meanwhile, he grabbed a hemp rake and jumped across to the other side of the tarn which had no bottom. «Come on, here I am!» cried Askeladden.

«Aren't there trees and logs there?» «Can't you hear there are no trees here,» said Askeladden, promising there were no trees or stumps. «Come on!»

So the troll started moving again. Splash! The troll landed in the tarn, and Askeladden hit him in the eyes with the rake each time he put his head above the surface.

The troll begged so pitifully for his life that the boy felt sorry for him, but first he had to renounce the princess and release the other one he had stolen previously, and promise that man and beast would be left in peace. Then the troll was allowed to creep home to his mountain.

THE WATERFALL SPIRIT

If you sit at the top of the waterfall, preferably on a bright moonlit evening, then you will hear and see the waterfall spirit. Down below in the black cauldron, amid the rings of frothing foam, he sits playing Nature's powerful melodies. At first it is only a thundering roar, but little by little it will take hold of you so that you want to throw yourself down into the music's echoing stream.

Here, all the songs ring out after lying in anxious silence in the woods and the mountains. All the voices of Nature ring forth from his strings, and the echo encircles all the sound, so that it rises as a single powerful chord.

The pine trees rustle, the aspen trees tremble, the brooks ripple and the birches quiver. In the mountain peaks the fresh winds rejoice, the silent forests sigh, and the still, deep forest tarn sings to the soft, melancholy strains of a willow flute. He bends over his fiddle, his bow moving back and forth in large, resounding movements. Everything must join in, step out over the precipice, into the whirlpool!

He plays with his eyes shut, looking into himself, standing in the midst of the tumult. Listen, he is keeping time with his foot!

His playing never ends. The glistening black cliffs rise to form a mighty temple within which the eternal tones can freely reverberate. High above, in the dark-blue vaults of the ceiling, hangs the silvery moon, reflected in glittering serpentine streaks in the deep black pools below.

Now the stars above are lit one by one. It is as if the strains grow wilder, as if every drop wishes to join the throngs and scatter its sparkle among them. But the strong, wild fiddler sits down there with his eyes closed, bent over his instrument. His own music is what binds him to his wet surroundings.

Then the eagle flew far away again, but then it grew tired and stopped in a pine tree. «Can you see something?» it asked.

«Well, I can't be certain,» said the man, «but I thought I could make out something in the distance.»
«Let's go a bit further, then,» said the eagle, taking to the air.
«Can you see anything now,» it asked after a while.
«Yes, he's right behind us now,» replied the man.
«You must let go of the boulder you picked up at the byre door,» said the eagle.

The man did this, and the boulder was turned into a high, black mountain peak, which Farmer Weatherbeard first had to force his way through. But when he came to the middle of the mountain, he broke one of his legs and had to go home to see to it.

While this was going on, the eagle took both the man and the hare home. When they got home, the man went to the churchyard and sprinkled consecrated earth on the hare, which turned it back into Hans, his son.

ON THE WAY TO THE FEAST
IN THE TROLL CASTLE

At last they were on the right road. Far away, above the dark wooded hills and the deep blue yonder, something resembling a star was twinkling. It quivered and shimmered with a strange radiance, sometimes white, then golden, then blue or green. The old trolls nodded to each other, for they knew they would find the way.

There was the troll castle.

The eyes of the young trolls grew wider and wider. They had never thought that anything so wonderful even existed. Oh, how fine, how splendid! Just imagine, the castle was made of gold. It glittered, reflected in the still, deep water, surrounded by pieces of silver floating and bobbing up and down. (…)

Over the great dark hills all around, the long procession of strange creatures came plodding. Some of them were so old that moss and small bushes were growing on them, others so ancient and bent with age that they resembled twisted pine roots and had to be carried. They creaked and groaned and rattled, they panted and snorted. They all wanted to get inside, amid the golden splendour, inside Soria Moria castle, which stood there shimmering with lights and ringing with music.

« W H A T   O N   E A R T H
W A S   T H A T ? »

Masterful use of the art of suggestion - which was not always Kittelsen's forte - is found in this colour sketch showing a tiny hut amid mounds of snow which has just escaped being trampled flat by a large troll, which we perceive only as a dark shadow vanishing over the hill. We feel the same trembling sensation, coupled with nervous laughter, which we always feel when human beings have a lucky escape from danger and dare to venture outside again and ask, their voices still trembling slightly, «What on earth was that?» Picture and text are inseparable here, both are essential to the meaning.

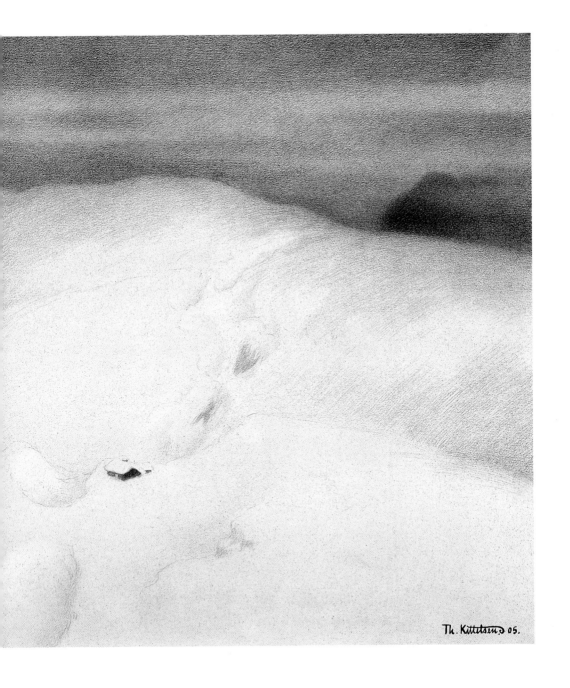

Th. Kittelsen 05.

THE MOUNTAIN
TROLL DIES

Behind the huge black cliff dwelt the mountain troll who burst in the sunlight. There, inside the mountain, he lay brooding in the dark over his piles of gold, silver and precious stones. The place shimmered and sparkled with treasures, and every time he moved, the gold tinkled.

Then he got to hear about the crock of gold in the sky, the sun, and he wanted it. Not to enjoy its rays, no, just to have it shut away in his big copper chest.

So one night he went out and blundered about, clearing stones from the slopes, hurling boulders and lumps of rock, bellowing and searching for the sun. Just think, how it would shine inside his copper box. He tossed and turned the stones to make thunder, and the lightning raged down the mountainside.

Far, far away, there seemed to be something shining between the peaks. It's not just any old rubbish that shines in the dark, so perhaps that's the sun, he thought. (...)

... The day starts to dawn. The light comes, slowly seeping. It will bring warmth, happiness, and nothing will be left out. Sorrow and gladness, joy and fear receive the same tender kiss. Rays of light know no hate.

Now the first sunbeam breaks forth above the dark outline of the mountains. (...)

He gritted his teeth in powerless rage and bit his evil tongues until the blood ran. His horny fingers tightened, his muscles and tendons stiffened like drawn bows.

Then the sun rose. He reeled, stumbled over, while the humble mountain flower in the crevice raised its cup to greet the day, brimming with a gleaming silvery dewdrop.

... Far below in the valley, where lights gleam from small windows, poor people dwell with little in the way of food or fuel. The winter is very hard and long, too long for poor folk. Just snow and wind, wind and snow ... And above them in the vast mountains, there are angry faces turned to stone. At night, in the darkness, they wander through people's dreams, frightening and menacing ...

GOBLIN WEDDING

From our old farm and alongside the river, which meandered in curves between charming little thickets, a large green field extended towards Solevatnet lake. Here and there stood small groups of fir trees, short, twisted pine trees, birches and alders, rowans and willows. Soft tufts of moss wandered like processions of goblins through the gently swirling evening mist - a fairytale, a strange, enchanting scene. The sad, pale goblin bride, in her gleaming silver headdress, was walking beside the ugly old Goblin King. A teeming throng of sneering, jeering grey spirits followed them in my imagination. I wanted to enter the realm of fantasy, of fairytales. - - Then the entire wedding procession vanished. But from the soft, greenish-brown clump of moss where I was sitting, thousands of small, graceful mayflies flew forth on their shining gauze wings. They settled all over my clothes, covering me entirely like the dew from the vanishing fairytale mist. Then they dropped down dead.

Theodor Kittelsen – painter, illustrator, author

NORWAY'S TROLL ARTIST

«We remember shuddering at his drawings of trolls, and the delights of childhood's fertile imagination come back to us, but as something now lost to us. The innocent Norway of the trolls is no more, and an artist such as Kittelsen would be unthinkable today. He is the lost country, our lost childhood. Perhaps we should see him as part of ourselves, from the days before writing, part of our rich illiterate inheritance before we learned to read.»

Theodor Kittelsen (1857–1914) is nowadays remembered and acknowledged by both Norwegians and foreigners as one of Norway's foremost illustrators of fairytales, and as the artist behind many of the most famous troll pictures in Asbjørnsen and Moe's collected folktales. His friend, the painter Christian Skredsvig, jokingly called him the «Lord High Troll Painter». The observations on the lost fairytale world of childhood and the indelible impression left by Kittelsen's illustrations of folktales and trolls on generations of Norwegian children are taken from Odd Hølaas' biography of Kittelsen, Den norske faun (The Norwegian Faun), written in 1959.

Folktale illustrator and social satirist

In this book, Hølaas describes how Kittelsen «had to stamp and shout to win recognition for his masterpieces. From his youth until his death, he fought against a tide of poverty and indifference. His main works were left fallow, or it might take up to four, even six years to find a publisher. He never had the chance to realise many of the great ideas he dreamed of.»

In Hølaas' view, Kittelsen was not exactly a happy character. His passionate, gloomy temperament contained dangerous forces. Kittelsen was sensitive and touchy, as great creative artists tend to be, given that they have to express themselves so forcefully. It is widely believed that Kittelsen's tempestuous, almost genius-like development came to a halt in the 1890s, and that he was a bitter man in later years.

Throughout his life, Kittelsen wanted to be an illustrator of books, but he was also an author of fairytales, fables, anecdotes, jokes and parodies. He was a noted social satirist, and with good-natured malice and merry disdain he impaled contemporary bourgeois society, the ruling classes and industrialists on his pen. His output was prolific and abundant and, as Holaas mentions, he never lived to see some of his book illustrations in print because no publisher was interested. It is paradoxical that a man who is nowadays one of Norway's most popular artists had to fight for recognition and a decent income throughout practically his entire artistic career.

In a letter written to a friend the first year the Kittelsen family was living at Lauvlia farm in Sigdal, he says, «It is often terribly difficult to be a Norwegian artist – so difficult that it sometimes seems hopeless. But it is no use being content with that notion. You have to pick yourself up and plod on. If I wasn't so fond of nature, of every flower in every stream, I don't know if I could manage it. But nature is a splendid consolation.»

The watchmaker's apprentice

Theodor Kittelsen was born in the coastal town of Kragerø and began his drawing career at an early age. The seafaring town of Kragerø must have been an exciting place for an imaginative, talented boy to grow up in. There were certainly plenty of people and scenes to provide inspiration here.

«There were adventures lurking in every nook and cranny of my native town. Funny old wooden buildings with mirrors at the windows, and high chimney-pots with rusty, creaking weathervanes. Old, slimy wells that groaned and moaned as soon as you touched the pump, narrow lanes and alleys running up and down the hill, and along the house walls grew dandelions, white nettle flowers, plantains and lush chickweed. Suddenly your foot would get trapped between the cobblestones, but there was no need to worry, because a horse and cart were as rare in Kragerø as a cow. Boats and sailing ships were the main thing. The harbour teemed with vessels from England, Germany, France, and the nice round Dutch smacks. If anyone asked a boy from Kragerø what he wanted to be, he would attract much mockery and shame if he did not immediately reply 'a sailor'.

«I was an exception, and my schoolmates tolerated this, because my drawing skills were much in demand. I even drew caricatures of my own strict teacher and sold them to his son for two big copper coins.»

Young Theodor's parents, however, were less enthusiastic about their son's inclination to become a painter, illustrator or sculptor. They wanted him to do something useful, and sent him to Arendal as an apprentice to a German-born watchmaker called Stein. Luckily for young Kittelsen, the watchmaker was a man who understood artistic talent. «You vill neffer be a vatchmaker in your leif, you are just sitting zere dreaming,» old Stein used to say. He put Kittelsen in touch with one of Arendal's wealthiest men, Diedrik Maria Aall, who lived in an old-fashioned manor house outside the town. This was to be the start of a patronage lasting many years.

One day Theodor Kittelsen, the watchmaker's apprentice, was sent to the manor house on an errand. «Shy and embarrassed, I went in feeling completely numb. But I was met by a kind, beaming face: Diedrik Maria Aall. 'Everything is arranged,' he said. 'You can leave for the Academy of Drawing in Kristiania as soon as you like.' I was trembling with emotion. I can remember his kind, sincere face to this day,» Kittelsen wrote in his memoirs «Folk og Trold. Minder og Drømme. Med Skizzer, Tegninger og Malerier» («People and Trolls. Memories and Dreams. With Sketches, Illustrations and Paintings»), published in 1911 in Copenhagen and Kristiania, as Norway's capital was known in those days.

Student life in Munich

After studying in Kristiania, Kittelsen moved to Munich, the bohemian city par excellence. According to Kittelsen's memoirs, «it teemed with artists in every corner, young academics with cocksure expressions, and rich, elegant artistic dandies, who were always accompanied by some vile mongrel dog with a gleaming collar and fancy lead. In their midst there would also appear strange, shabby, fantastic creatures with tall, wide-brimmed bowler hats, long hair down to their shoulders, and a miserable scrap of plaid draped loosely round them. Fat beer connoisseurs, who no doubt valued Bier und Rindfleisch more highly than art, talked noisily and gesticulated wildly with their arms. Students in elegant uniforms with silly, blotchy faces threw aggressive glances in all directions. Aristocratic, red-haired English misses displayed their Venus-like figures through thin silk dresses, and poor Italian artist's models smiled and laughed; they wore their bohemian rags with more dignity and grace than anyone else. (...)

«The Academy of Fine Arts, where I immediately became a student of one of the most gifted professors, was a mixing place for all the world's nations, where

strange tongues from all over the world were spoken. But we were all the best of friends, regardless of nationality, poverty or prosperity.»

In «Den norske Faun», Kittelsen's biographer Odd Hølaas writes that, even during his time in Munich, Kittelsen had begun to display his determined obstinacy. He could not emulate the masterly virtuosity of his fellow painters, nor did he wish to. Kittelsen was not an academic artist, but a folk artist, who many years later would find expression for his talents in the fields he liked best, as a lyrical painter of nature and illustrator of folktales. «The others were able to unfold their wings and fly towards a common goal, according to common instinct, towards new artistic territory, whereas Kittelsen's journey begins with a completely

different image: the crab retreating backwards from the wider world, constantly making for home, more of a resolute realist than the others and with much, much more imagination.»

Kittelsen himself describes his long conversations with a Finnish art student, a clergyman's son from Kuopio, who became his best friend during his studies in Munich. As they drank beer and ate German sausage during breaks at the Academy, «we constantly talked and dreamed about nature at home. We were equally enthusiastic: Norway and Finland were the most beautiful countries of all!»

Theodor Kittelsen spend several happy periods in Munich and Paris among fellow foreign and Norwegian artists such as Harriet Backer, Eilif Petterssen, Erik Werenskiold and Christian Skredsvig, but his financial straits forced his friends and well-wishers at home in Norway to come to his rescue, and a bank loan enabled the young illustrator and painter to return to Norway in 1880.

Happy years at Lauvlia

After his studies in Munich and Paris, Theodor Kittelsen led a rather unsettled and itinerant existence with his wife Inga and their children, who eventually numbered nine. They moved from place to place in Norway, spending their longest and perhaps happiest time at Lauvlia farm in Sigdal, where they moved in 1900. This is where many of the illustrations to Asbjørnsen and Moe's collection of Norwegian folktales were drawn.

Kittelsen describes life at Lauv-lia and his constant financial worries in a letter to a friend, saying, «At last it looks as if summer is coming. This winter has been a nightmare for me, as dark and dreary as it could possibly be. But now the catkins are beginning to appear, and it seems as if the heart and mind are starting to lighten. I am longing to get up into the mountains, where I have some lovely things waiting for me – so lovely, in fact, that I can hardly bear to think about them. Last year I was too preoccupied with money troubles to cope with this house, so I didn't stray far. I am expecting a different outcome this summer.

«I am very fond of my little studio – this is the first time I have had my working room arranged neatly and tidily the way I want it. The house is in a delightful position – summer here is absolutely beautiful. We live in the middle of a birch wood, which slopes down towards Lake Soneren. My one wish is that we are allowed to keep it, and that I can finish working on it. It is not large, but in time I shall make it into a real little fairytale home. My wife and I do most of the work ourselves – I carve, paint and decorate, she can weave and sew, as befits a poor princess who has been captured by a troll. And then there are the children – I'm almost losing count of them – our five children. Every time I visit Kristiania (which is not very often), my distinguished colleagues tell me I have too many, so I hardly dare venture there any more – I am trying my best to conceal myself and the children behind bushes and rocks. It has never occurred to me that I have too many.

«Yes, things can certainly be hard sometimes, but in summer the Good Lord always provides us with an ample measure of potatoes, and the cowberries grow beside the road.

«And in summer, my wife and I have to go fishing. We put out nets and catch mainly perch, which is full of nasty bones that easily get lodged in your throat. Eventually we lose our nets, so we stop.

«That's what life is like up here – as you see, there is plenty of variety.

«But the capercaillies cavort in the dark pine woods, where you can smell bears, and down in the black lake, the water-sprite lies in wait in the evenings.»

Ten years later, the family was forced to sell up and move.

Emotional tension and fear of nature

Scholars have suggested that Theodor Kittelsen used images of nature to make the case for being alone. The need for solitude is a powerful theme in Kittelsen's works, according to the Norwegian author Einar Økland. In an article in the literary journal Basar (No. 4, 1976), he writes: «One might wonder whether people in Norway are not largely solitary anyway, and whether there is a need for more solitude.

«There may well be. Being alone with a piece of remote nature is probably a means of liberation. Nature is something we have to fight against if we are to survive, but it is also something we can approach by stealth, observe and think what we like about. For one thing, we can populate nature with the products of our imagination.»

That was exactly what Kittelsen did, in masterly fashion. He was probably intensely in love with nature. «The message he conveys in words and pictures is that it is possible to perceive nature accurately and sharply, while allowing room for the great emotions that fill the entire soul when you stand face to face with it. (…) Kittelsen's depictions were bold and sharp.»

Einar Økland believes it is the suggestive element in Kittelsen's art that attracts us to it and makes us bother with it in the first place. We recognise the tension and drama as our own emotions and tensions. He is in no doubt that there is much fear behind Kittelsen's works.

To support his case, he cites Kittelsen's close friend, the painter Christian Skredsvig, who wrote on one occasion that the melancholy Norwegian countryside was where Kittelsen met the trolls and the goblins. «The great forests were teeming with them. Incidentally, I don't believe Kittelsen ever ventured in there; he was scared of nature. At root, it was probably his fear of the vastness and silence of nature and humanity that gave his art its strange mysticism. He never got any further than the edge of the forest before meeting all the remarkable beings that are so familiar to us from his drawings.

THE FOREST TROLL
From: Trollskap - Theodor Kittelsen i tekst, tegninger og malerier, Gyldendal Norsk Forlag, Oslo 1957

THE SMALL BOYS WHO MET THE TROLLS OF HEDAL FOREST
From: Asbjørnsen og Moes samlede eventyr, Vol. II, Gyldendal Norsk Forlag, Oslo 1965

THE THREE PRINCESSES IN THE BLUE MOUNTAIN
From: Asbjørnsen og Moes samlede eventyr, Vol. II, Gyldendal Norsk Forlag, Oslo 1965

THE GOLDEN BIRD
From: Asbjørnsen og Moes samlede eventyr, Vol. II, Gyldendal Norsk Forlag, Oslo 1965

THE BLUE RIBBON
From: Asbjørnsen og Moes samlede eventyr, Vol. III, Gyldendal Norsk Forlag, Oslo 1965

VESLEFRIKK AND HIS FIDDLE
From: Asbjørnsen og Moes samlede eventyr, Vol. II, Gyldendal Norsk Forlag, Oslo 1965

THE FAIRIES
From: Trollskap - Theodor Kittelsen i tekst, tegninger og malerier, Gyldendal Norsk Forlag, Oslo 1957

ASKELADDEN STEALS THE TROLL'S PIECES OF SILVER, BEDSPREAD AND GOLDEN HARP
From: Asbjørnsen and Moe, Jomfrua på Glassberget og andre eventyr, Aschehoug, Oslo 1949

SORIA MORIA CASTLE
From: Asbjørnsen og Moes samlede eventyr, Vol. II, Gyldendal Norsk Forlag, Oslo 1965

ASKELADDEN'S EATING CONTEST WITH THE TROLL
From: Asbjørnsen og Moes samlede eventyr, Vol. II, Gyldendal Norsk Forlag, Oslo 1965

POLAR BEAR KING VALEMON
From: Asbjørnsen og Moes samlede eventyr, Vol. II, Gyldendal Norsk Forlag, Oslo 1965

THE PIXIE
From: Trollskap - Theodor Kittelsen i tekst, tegninger og malerier. Gyldendal Norsk Forlag, Oslo 1957

PEER GYNT IN THE HALL OF THE MOUNTAIN KING
From: Henrik Ibsen, Peer Gynt, Fakkel-bok, Gyldendal Norsk Forlag, Oslo 1962

BUTTERBALL
From: Asbjørnsen og Moes samlede eventyr, Vol. II, Gyldendal Norsk Forlag, Oslo 1965

THE WATER-SPRITE
From: Trollskap - Theodor Kittelsen i tekst, tegninger og malerier. Gyldendal Norsk Forlag, Oslo 1957

THE HEN DANCING IN THE MOUNTAIN
From: Asbjørnsen and Moe, Jomfrua på Glassberget og andre eventyr, Aschehoug, Oslo 1949

RED FOX AND ASKELADDEN
From: Asbjørnsen og Moes samlede eventyr, Vol. II, Gyldendal Norsk Forlag, Oslo 1965

THE WATERFALL SPIRIT
From: Trollskap - Theodor Kittelsen i tekst, tegninger og malerier. Gyldendal Norsk Forlag, Oslo 1957

FARMER WEATHERBEARD
From: Asbjørnsen og Moes samlede eventyr, Vol. II, Gyldendal Norsk Forlag, Oslo 1965

ON THE WAY TO THE FEAST IN THE TROLL CASTLE
From: Trollskap - Theodor Kittelsen i tekst, tegninger og malerier. Gyldendal Norsk Forlag, Oslo 1957

«WHAT ON EARTH WAS THAT?»
From: Leif Østby, Theodor Kittelsen - Tegninger og akvareller, Dreyers Forlag 1975

THE MOUNTAIN TROLL DIES
From: Trollskap - Theodor Kittelsen i tekst, tegninger og malerier, Gyldendal Norsk Forlag, Oslo 1957

GOBLIN WEDDING
From: Theodor Kittelsen, Folk og Trold, Minder og Drømme. Med Skizzer, Tegninger og Malerier, Kristiania/Copenhagen, Gyldendalske Boghandel/Nordisk Forlag 1911

© Egmont Bøker Fredhøi AS – SFG
N-0055 Oslo
Tel: +47 22 47 11 50
Fax: +47 22 47 11 74
E-mail: sfg@egmont.no
Internet: www.touristbooks.com

Author/Editor: Per Erik Borge
Translations: Berlitz GlobalNET
Photography: O. Væring, National Gallery Oslo
Design: Skomsøy Grønli AS
Printed in Denmark by Nørhaven AS